DECODING PERSONAL FINANCE

A DIY HANDBOOK

ROHIT NAYAR

notionpress.com

INDIA • SINGAPORE • MALAYSIA

Contents

Acknowledgements

Writing **Decoding Personal Finance** has been a rewarding journey that would not have been possible without the support and encouragement of many remarkable individuals.

First and foremost, I would like to express my deepest gratitude to my family. My beautiful wife, son, and my parents. Your unwavering love, patience, and understanding provided me with the strength and determination to see this project through to completion. To my friends and colleagues, thank you for your insightful feedback, stimulating discussions, and constant encouragement.

I want to give special thanks to my mentors and teachers, who have imparted valuable knowledge and wisdom over the years, especially My Father, Mr. Ram Nayar. Your guidance has been instrumental in my personal and professional development.

I would also like to extend my appreciation to the financial experts and practitioners who contributed their insights and experiences, enhancing the practical value of this book.

Lastly, to my readers, thank you for your interest in **Decoding Personal Finance**. I hope this book serves as a valuable resource on your journey to financial literacy and empowerment.

With heartfelt gratitude,

Rohit Nayar

Prologue

Imagine a life where money isn't a source of stress but a tool to achieve your dreams. In the vast world of personal finance, understanding how money works is key to unlocking a better life filled with dreams and aspirations. Yet, the journey to financial empowerment can be confusing and even intimidating. That's where "Decoding Personal Finance" comes in. This book tackles your daily money questions and provides clear answers, guiding you towards financial freedom and security.

"Decoding Personal Finance" is designed to turn complex financial concepts into easy-to-understand lessons. From mastering the basics of budgeting to exploring advanced investment strategies, each chapter is a stepping stone towards financial independence. It's crafted for anyone who earns or will soon start earning, recognising the unique challenges and opportunities in our diverse world.

Our mission is to make personal finance accessible and understandable for everyone. This book isn't just a guide; it's a companion on your journey to financial literacy. We know taking control of your financial future can feel overwhelming, but each chapter is designed to build your confidence and help you navigate the financial landscape with ease.

Picture a future where you have the knowledge and confidence to make wise financial decisions. Whether you're saving for your child's education, building a nest egg for retirement, or investing in opportunities that align with your values, this book will help you turn those dreams into reality.

Let's be clear: this isn't about quick fixes or overnight wealth. True financial empowerment requires dedication, patience, and a lifelong commitment to learning and growth. It's about understanding the principles of personal finance, developing healthy financial habits, and making choices that align with your goals and values.

Throughout this book, we'll discuss essential components of a personal financial plan, from managing money basics to setting goals, creating budgets, investing wisely, protecting your assets, and planning for the future. Each chapter equips you with the knowledge and tools you need to tackle personal finance with confidence.

"Decoding Personal Finance" is a call to action. It's about taking charge of your financial destiny, engaging with the material, reflecting on your own financial situation, and embracing the opportunity for growth. Personal finance isn't a one-size-fits-all approach. Your journey is uniquely shaped by your circumstances, values, and aspirations. This book helps you create a financial plan that resonates with your life's purpose, empowering you to apply its insights and strategies to your specific needs and goals.

As we embark on this journey together, let's embrace the power within us to take control of our financial future. Let's make informed choices and create a life of abundance, armed with knowledge, and guided by wisdom. The time to unlock your financial potential is now. Are you ready to master personal financial planning? Let's begin.

How To Get the Most out of This Book

"Decoding Personal Finance" is designed to be a practical guide that empowers you to take control of your financial future. To make the most of this book and maximise its benefits, consider the following tips:

- **Read with Intent:** Approach each chapter with an open and curious mindset. Take the time to absorb the information and reflect on how it applies to your personal financial situation.

- **Take Notes:** Jot down key concepts, strategies, and ideas that resonate with you. This will help you remember and revisit important information later on.

- **Reflect on Your Financial Goals:** As you progress through the chapters, reflect on your own financial goals and aspirations. Consider how the concepts discussed can help you achieve those goals and adapt the strategies to fit your circumstances.

- **Apply the Knowledge:** Knowledge alone is not enough; action is key. Identify specific steps you can take based on the information in each chapter. Start implementing the strategies and principles discussed to see tangible improvements in your financial well-being.

- **Seek Additional Guidance:** While this book provides a comprehensive overview of personal financial planning, it's essential to recognise that every individual's situation is unique. Consider consulting with a qualified financial adviser who can provide personalised advice tailored to your specific needs and goals.

- **Share and Discuss:** Engage in conversations about personal finance with friends, family, or like-minded individuals. Share insights from the book on your social media and discuss different perspectives. This can enhance your understanding and motivate you to stay committed to your financial goals.

- **Stay Committed:** Remember that personal financial planning is a long-term commitment. It requires discipline, consistency, and periodic reassessment. Stay dedicated to your financial journey, and be open to learning and adapting along the way.

Chapter 1

Understanding the Basics of Personal Finance

In this chapter, we lay the foundation for personal financial planning from the perspective of a complete layperson.

1.1   Income and Expenses

Income is simply money which comes to your pocket, and expense is money which goes out of your pocket. Income refers to the money you receive or earn, typically through various sources such as employment, investments, or allowances. It is the amount of money flowing into your pocket.

For example, let's consider a high school student named Lakshmi. Lakshmi works part-time at a local bookstore after college, earning a monthly income of ₹5,000. This money represents Lakshmi's income, which she can use for various purposes.

Expenses, on the other hand, refer to the money you spend or use to pay for goods, services, or other financial obligations. Expenses include buying food, paying for transportation, purchasing clothes, and paying bills.

Continuing with our example, Lakshmi has certain expenses she needs to cover each month. She spends ₹1,000 on transportation to get to and from work and college. She allocates ₹1,500 for groceries and personal care items. Lakshmi also has a monthly phone bill of ₹500, and she sets aside ₹500 for leisure activities and entertainment. These expenses represent the money that Lakshmi needs to spend to meet her various needs and desires, all in rupees.

To summarise:

- Income: The money Lakshmi earns from her part-time job at the bookstore, which is ₹5,000 per month.

- Expenses: The money Lakshmi spends covers different aspects of her life. This includes ₹1,000 for transportation, ₹1,500 for groceries, ₹500 for her phone bill, and ₹500 for leisure activities.

Understanding the concepts of income and expenses is important because it allows individuals to track their financial inflows and outflows on a daily basis. By effectively managing their income and expenses, individuals can make informed decisions about how to allocate their money, ensure they are living within their means, and work towards their financial goals.

For a college student like Lakshmi, being aware of her income and expenses helps her make choices about how to prioritise and allocate her money. It also encourages her to develop good money management habits from an early age, setting a foundation for future financial success.

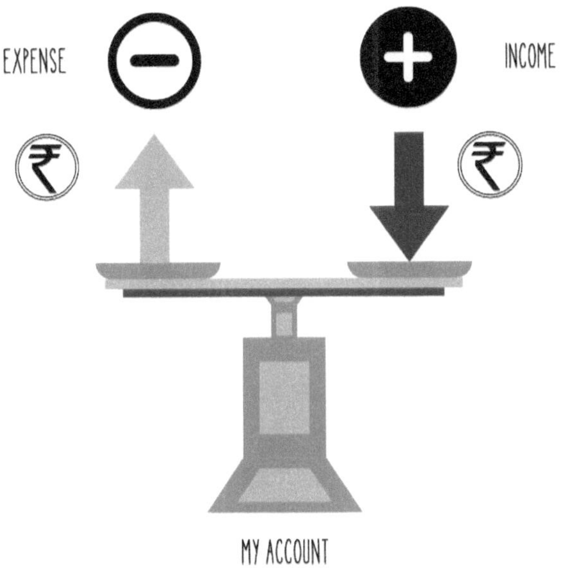

1.2 Assets and Liabilities

Rohan, a hardworking individual, is employed in a corporate job and earns a steady income.'He owns a 2BHK apartment valued at 80 lakh rupees. This apartment serves as an asset for Rohan as it has a market value and provides him with rental income. Rohan rents out the apartment, generating a monthly rental income of 15,000 rupees. The apartment contributes positively to Rohan's financial well-being by providing a steady stream of income.

Now, let's consider Rohan's decision to purchase a new investment property – another 2BHK apartment valued at

80 lakh rupees. Rohan makes a downpayment of 15 lakh rupees from his savings and decides to avail a home loan to cover the remaining amount.

In this case:

- Asset: Rohan's first 2BHK apartment is valued at 80 lakh rupees, which generates a monthly rental income of 15,000 rupees.

- Liability: Rohan's new investment property, for which he made a downpayment of 15 lakh rupees and availed a home loan to cover the remaining amount. The loan represents a financial obligation or liability as Rohan is required to make regular repayments, including the principal and interest, to the bank or financial institution.

The new investment property, although also an asset due to its market value and potential for rental income, carries a liability in the form of the home loan that Rohan has taken to finance its purchase.

It's important for Rohan to assess the potential rental income, expenses, and cash flow associated with the new investment property to ensure it aligns with his financial goals. By effectively managing both assets and liabilities, Rohan can work towards building a diversified property portfolio, generating rental income, and growing his net worth.

Understanding the concepts of assets and liabilities helps individuals like Rohan make informed financial decisions, evaluate the impact of their investments, determine the amount of loan repayment EMI they pay, and effectively manage their personal finances.

1.3   Power of Compounding

Investing is often described as a journey, and the power of compounding serves as the vehicle propelling us toward financial success. As we delve into the world of compounding, it becomes evident that time is indeed money, and the earlier one starts, the more profound the impact. Let's unravel the mysteries of compounding and understand how it can shape your financial future.

Understanding the Power of Compounding

At its core, compounding is the process where the value of an investment grows exponentially over time. Unlike simple interest, which is calculated only on the principal amount, compound interest takes into account both the principal and the accumulated interest. This compounding effect is the secret sauce behind the remarkable success stories of seasoned investors.

The Formula Behind Compounding

The compounding formula is elegantly simple yet holds immense power. It involves the principal amount, the interest rate, and the time the money is invested. The longer the money compounds, the more significant the impact, showcasing the symbiotic relationship between time and compounding.

Real Life Examples of Compounding

History is replete with examples of individuals who harnessed the power of compounding to amass great wealth. From legendary investors to everyday savers, stories abound of how even modest investments grew into substantial fortunes over time. These examples serve as both inspiration and a testament to the magic of compounding.

Warren Buffett, often regarded as one of the most successful investors of our time, attributes much of his success to the power of compounding. His journey from a young investor with a fascination for numbers to the chairman and CEO of Berkshire Hathaway is a testament to the enduring impact of compounding in the world of finance. Warren Buffett is often quoted saying, "The best time to plant a tree was 20 years ago. The second-best time is now." This encapsulates his belief in the paramount importance of starting early in the realm of investing. Buffett's own journey reflects the profound impact that time can have on compounding. Buffett hasn't bought any additional Coca-Cola shares since 1988, meaning the growth is almost entirely due to the power of compounding. By reinvesting the dividends, he continually increased his number of shares, which led to larger dividends, which led to more reinvested shares, and so on. It's like a financial perpetual motion machine.

Another compelling example is Buffett's investment in American Express. Purchased in the early 1990s, Buffett's initial 10% stake in the company has grown to about 20%, largely due to the dividends he's received and reinvested. Again, it's the music of compound interest playing to his tune.

Start Early, Benefit More

One of the golden rules of investing is to start early. The concept of time in the market is more important than timing the market is rooted in the idea that the longer your money is invested, the more it can benefit from compounding. Comparisons between those who started investing in their 20s versus their 40s reveal a stark contrast in the final outcomes.

The Role of Consistency in Compounding

Consistency is the unsung hero of compounding. Regular contributions to your investment portfolio, no matter how small, can accumulate into substantial wealth over time. It's not about the size of the investment but the steadfast commitment to the process.

Compounding in Different Investment Vehicles

Compounding isn't exclusive to a particular investment type. Whether it's stocks, bonds, whole life insurance policies or mutual funds, the principle of compounding remains constant. Diversifying across these vehicles can enhance the overall compounded growth and mitigate risks associated with a single investment class.

Understanding Risks and Returns

While the allure of high returns is undeniable, understanding and managing risks is crucial in the world of compounding. Striking a balance between risk and return ensures that the compounding journey is smooth and resilient to market fluctuations.

The Psychological Aspect of Compounding

Patience is a virtue in investing, and compounding magnifies the importance of this quality. Overcoming the temptation for short-term gains and staying focused on long-term objectives is the key to unlocking the full potential of compounding.

Compounding and Retirement Planning

Compounding is a reliable ally in retirement planning. By strategically allocating investments with an eye on the long-term, individuals can build a nest egg that supports a comfortable retirement lifestyle.

In conclusion, the power of compounding is a force to be reckoned with in the world of investing. Starting early, staying consistent, and understanding the nuances of compounding are the pillars of financial success. As you embark on your investment journey, remember that compounding is not a sprint but a marathon, and the rewards are well worth the patience and dedication.

In the heart of India, nestled among the ancient temples, was a small village called Mangalpur. A humble school teacher named Arjun lived in this village. Arjun was known for his wisdom and his knack for explaining complex concepts through simple, engaging stories.

One evening, under the shade of the banyan tree, Arjun gathered the village children and adults alike. With a twinkle in his eye, he began, "Today, I shall tell you a story about the magic of compounding in investments, a story that can turn the ordinary into the extraordinary."

The crowd leaned in, curious. Arjun continued, "In the times long past, there was a young man named Ravi. Ravi inherited a small sum of money from his grandfather, a mere 1,000 rupees. Unsure of what to do with it, Ravi sought the counsel of an old sage who lived atop the hill overlooking the village."

"The sage welcomed Ravi and listened to his predicament. He then handed Ravi a single grain of rice and said, 'Invest this grain wisely and let it grow.' Perplexed, Ravi returned home, pondering the sage's words."

"As days turned into weeks, Ravi remembered the sage's advice. He decided to invest his 1,000 rupees in a small plot of land where he planted crops. With each harvest, he reinvested his earnings into buying more land and better seeds. Years passed, and Ravi's diligence bore fruit. His small investment began to grow, and soon, he was one of the wealthiest men in the region."

Arjun paused, letting the weight of the story sink in. "But here lies the true magic. Ravi didn't just earn and spend. He reinvested his gains, allowing his wealth to grow exponentially. This, my friends, is the power of compounding."

He picked up a small stick and drew circles in the dirt. "Imagine, if you will, this circle represents your initial investment. With each reinvestment, your wealth doesn't just grow; it multiplies. It's like planting a tree. The first seed grows into a sapling, the sapling into a tree, and the tree bears fruits that contain more seeds."

Arjun's eyes sparkled as he spoke. "In India, we have a tradition of saving, but to truly harness the magic of compounding, one must invest wisely and patiently. Just as Ravi turned a grain of rice into a fortune, so too can we turn our modest savings into substantial wealth."

The villagers nodded, inspired by the tale. They understood that the key to financial growth was not just in saving but in reinvesting and allowing their wealth to compound over time. Arjun concluded with a smile, "Remember, the magic of compounding is a powerful ally. Use it wisely, and you will see your fortunes grow beyond your wildest dreams."

Let's explore an example of saving 1.2 lakh rupees per year for 15 years at a compounding rate of 12%. We can calculate the future value of these savings.

Each year, the individual saves 1.2 lakh rupees, resulting in a total savings of 18 lakhs over 15 years. At a compounding rate of 12%, the money grows exponentially. Using a compound interest calculator, we find that after 15 years, the savings would reach approximately 50.4 lakhs.

This illustrates how disciplined savings combined with the power of compounding can significantly grow wealth over time. It's important to note that compounding returns can vary depending on market conditions and investment performance. The example assumes a constant compounding rate of 12% for illustrative purposes.

By leveraging the principles of compounding and disciplined savings, individuals can build a substantial corpus for various financial goals, such as retirement, education, or property purchase.

1.4 Let Us Now Understand How to Have a Strong Financial Foundation.

Once upon a time, in a small coastal village, there lived a wise fisherman named Ram. Ram had spent his entire life fishing in the abundant seas surrounding his village. Despite having a modest income, Ram had managed to build a strong financial foundation for himself and his family.

Here's how Ram established his strong financial foundation:

- **Emergency Fund:** Ram understood the importance of being prepared for unexpected circumstances. Over the years, he diligently saved a portion of his income and built an emergency fund. This fund provided a safety net for him and his family during times of unforeseen expenses or financial emergencies. For instance, when Ram's fishing boat needed urgent repairs after a storm, he had the necessary funds readily available in his emergency fund.

- **Insurance:** Recognising the risks associated with his profession, Ram ensured that he had adequate insurance coverage. He purchased health insurance to protect against medical expenses and disability insurance to safeguard his income in case of injury. Ram also insured his fishing equipment and boat to mitigate potential losses due to accidents or natural disasters. He also bought life insurance = 10 times his annual income to safeguard against loss of income in case of an unforeseen event.

- **Debt Management:** Ram was careful about managing his debts. He never borrowed excessively and made timely repayments on any loans he had taken for business purposes. His EMI never went more than 30% of his monthly income. By being mindful of his debt obligations, Ram avoided falling into a debt trap and maintained a healthy financial position.

- ***Savings and Investments:*** Despite his modest income, Ram prioritised saving a portion of his earnings. He set aside 20% of his income regularly and invested it wisely to grow his wealth. Ram sought advice from financial professionals and diversified his investments, including investing in mutual funds, stocks, pension funds and fixed deposits. Through consistent savings and prudent investments, Ram saw his wealth gradually grow over time.

- ***Future Planning:*** Ram understood the importance of planning for the future. He allocated a portion of his savings towards long-term goals, such as educating his children and securing a comfortable retirement. Ram regularly reviewed his financial plan and adjusted it as necessary to stay on track.

By establishing a strong financial foundation, Ram was able to weather financial storms, protect his family's well-being, and pursue his long-term goals. He had the peace of mind that comes from knowing he had taken steps to secure his financial future.

* * *

What did we learn so far from chapter 1:

1. _______________________________________

____

____

____

2. _______________________________________

____

____

____

3. _______________________________________

____

____

____

Note:

To deepen your understanding of the concepts covered in this chapter, please take the time to answer the following questions. Reflect on what you have learned and provide written responses to the open-ended questions. This exercise is designed to reinforce your knowledge and encourage you to apply the principles to your own financial planning.

What are my sources of income?

What are my liabilities as of date?

What possible financial emergencies can I face?

What investments am I making today that use the power of compounding?

Do I have a plan in place to receive fixed passive income if I retire tomorrow?

Chapter 2

Setting Financial Goals & Objectives

Before we touch on the topic of financial goals, let's understand what goals are and their importance in general. In the journey of life, goals are the threads that weave our dreams into reality. Jim Rohn, the masterful philosopher of personal development, often spoke about success not as a destination to be reached but as a journey to be experienced. At the very heart of this transformative journey lies the concept of goals.

Jim's teachings echo the profound truth that success is not a random occurrence; it is attracted by the person we become. This concept revolutionises the way we perceive our goals. They are not mere endpoints; rather, they are the guiding stars that lead us to self-discovery and personal evolution.

2.1 Goals

Goals are, in essence, the blueprints of our dreams. They provide structure to our ambitions, offering a clear and defined path toward realising our desires. When we set goals, we initiate a process of growth and development that extends beyond the achievement of the goal itself.

One of Jim Rohn's fundamental insights is that the pursuit of success is, in reality, the pursuit of personal development. The journey towards our goals transforms us. It shapes our character, hones our skills, and refines our mindset. In setting and striving for goals, we become architects of our destiny, actively participating in the creation of the person we are meant to be.

Clarity, according to Jim, is the linchpin of this transformation. To attract success, one must be clear about what they want and why they want it. This level of clarity acts as a powerful force, propelling individuals forward with a sense of purpose and direction. Without a clear destination, the journey becomes aimless, and success remains an elusive mirage.

Consider the analogy of a ship at sea. Without a destination plotted on the map, the ship may sail endlessly, tossed by the unpredictable currents. Goals act as the North Star, providing sailors with a fixed point of reference guiding them through stormy seas and uncharted waters. Similarly, our goals guide us through the uncertainties of life, offering a constant reference point in the ever-changing landscape of challenges and opportunities.

The power of goals lies not only in their ability to guide but also in their capacity to inspire. Jim Rohn believed that the goals we set should be big, audacious, and aligned with our deepest desires. A lofty goal, he argued, serves as a magnet, drawing out the latent potential within us. It sparks creativity, fuels determination, and propels us to surpass our perceived limitations.

In the realm of personal development, the journey is as significant as the destination. Jim often used the metaphor of the acorn to illustrate this point. Within the tiny acorn resides the mighty oak tree, but the acorn must undergo a process of growth, facing the challenges of the soil, weathering storms, and reaching towards the sun. Similarly, our goals are the acorns of our potential, and the journey toward them is the process that transforms us into the towering oaks of success.

To fully grasp the significance of goals, we must recognise that success is not an event but a continuous evolution. The achievement of one goal is merely a milestone in the larger journey of personal development. Jim Rohn encouraged individuals to view their goals as a series of stepping stones, each leading to a higher level of achievement and fulfilment.

Now, let's talk about inspiration. Jim Rohn was all about setting big, audacious goals. So, don't settle for pocket change—dream big! If you're thinking of a goal, ask yourself, "Is this goal inspiring enough to get me out of bed in the morning?" If it doesn't give you that "heck yeah!" feeling, it might be time to dream a little bigger.

Remember the ship analogy? Without a destination, you're just floating around. Well, think of your financial goal as the treasure island you want to reach. Maybe it's saving a certain amount of money, investing, or starting a side hustle. Your goal becomes the North Star, guiding you through the ocean of financial choices and helping you steer clear of money storms.

Now, let's talk about the journey. Jim Rohn loved the idea that success isn't just about reaching the goal; it's about who you become along the way. Applying this to money matters means that the process of saving, investing, and hustling for your financial goals is just as important as hitting the money target.

Now, let's tie it all together. Your financial goals are like the seeds you plant in the garden of your dreams. Each goal is a tiny acorn that, with care and attention, grows into a mighty oak of financial success. Picture it: your financial garden, with money trees bearing the fruit of your hard work and smart choices.

2.2　Goals one can have with age.

Here are a few general financial goals one can have as they progress with age:

Age 25-30:

- Paying off student loans or any high-interest debt

- Saving for a down payment on a home or considering rental investments

- Investing in skill development or further education for career advancement

- Saving for a wedding or funding major life events

Age 30-35:

- Purchasing a new home or upgrading to a larger property

- Expanding investment portfolios

- Planning for children's education and setting up education funds

- Reviewing and adjusting insurance coverage (life, health, and property)

Age 35-40:

- Balancing multiple financial goals, such as retirement, children's education, and mortgage payments

- Accelerating retirement savings and maximising contributions to retirement accounts

- Exploring entrepreneurship or starting a business

- Reevaluating career choices and long-term income potential

Age 40-50:

- Ensuring mortgage payments are on track for early repayment

- Supporting children's higher education expenses

- Preparing for potential healthcare costs and long-term care insurance. Assessing retirement readiness and making necessary adjustments

- Creating a comprehensive estate plan, including wills and trusts

Age 50 and above:

- Transitioning from full-time work to part-time or retirement

- Consolidating retirement accounts and optimising withdrawals

- Estate planning and creating a legacy for future generations

- Implementing tax-efficient strategies for income and investments

- Prioritising health and wellness, including adequate insurance coverage

You might be wondering how these goals will be met and what financial instruments to use to do so. We will be covering that in the following chapters.

Remember, individual circumstances and priorities can vary, so this list serves as a general guide. It's important to customise financial goals based on personal aspirations, income, family dynamics, and lifestyle choices. Regularly reviewing and adjusting goals with the help of financial advisers can ensure alignment with changing circumstances and optimise financial well-being.

Once upon a time, a farmer named Rajesh lived in a small village in India. Rajesh owned a modest piece of land where he cultivated crops to support his family. Despite his hard work and dedication, Rajesh often faced financial difficulties due to a lack of financial planning. In the early years, Rajesh focused solely on farming and neglected to set financial goals or establish a budget. He didn't keep track of his expenses or income, and as a result, he struggled to manage his finances effectively.

During one particular farming season, Rajesh encountered an unexpected drought that severely impacted his crop yield. Without a contingency plan or savings, he found himself unable to cover the expenses needed to sustain his family and continue farming. Rajesh was forced to borrow money from local lenders at high-interest rates, creating a cycle of debt that became increasingly difficult to escape.

The lack of financial planning also affected Rajesh's ability to invest in his farming practices. He couldn't afford modern equipment or machinery that could have improved his productivity and yielded better crop results. As a result, his income remained stagnant while his expenses continued to rise.

Over time, Rajesh realised the importance of financial planning. He sought guidance from financial advisers. Rajesh learned to set financial goals, create a budget, and establish an emergency fund.

With newfound knowledge and discipline, Rajesh started implementing these financial strategies. He allocated a portion of his earnings towards savings, built an emergency fund in the next 12 months for unexpected situations, and began investing in his farm by purchasing better-quality seeds and adopting more efficient farming techniques.

As the years passed, it took him 5 years to recover from the losses he made that one bad year, and Rajesh's financial situation gradually improved. He experienced better crop yields, reduced his debt burden, and managed to save for his children's education. Rajesh's newfound financial planning skills also allowed him to weather economic fluctuations and navigate challenging times with greater resilience.

Through his journey, Rajesh realised the importance of financial planning in providing stability and security for himself and his family. He shared his experiences with fellow farmers in the village, encouraging them to embrace financial planning and set goals to improve their financial well-being.

Remember, whether one is a farmer or engaged in any other profession, financial planning can make a substantial difference in navigating life's uncertainties and achieving long-term financial stability.

Let Us Now Understand What Not Having Goals Could Lead Us to:

- **Lack of Direction and Purpose:** Without setting financial goals, we may lack a clear sense of direction and purpose when it comes to our finances. We may find ourselves aimlessly drifting through financial decisions, making impulsive choices, and missing out on opportunities to achieve our aspirations.

- **Missed Opportunities:** Planning for future financial goals allows us to identify and seize opportunities for growth and prosperity. Without a plan, we may overlook investments, savings strategies, or career choices that could have significantly impacted our financial well-being in the long run.

- **Financial Stress and Instability:** Without planning, we may face financial stress and instability. Emergencies, unexpected expenses, or changes in circumstances can catch us off guard, leaving us ill-prepared to handle them. This can lead to financial strain, debt accumulation, and a constant state of financial insecurity.

- **Inadequate Retirement Planning:** Neglecting to plan for retirement can have serious consequences. It may result in insufficient savings to sustain our desired lifestyle in our later years. Without a retirement plan, we may need to rely on external support or work longer than anticipated, limiting our ability to enjoy the freedom and relaxation that retirement can offer.

- **Limited Wealth Accumulation:** Planning for financial goals allows us to take advantage of the power of compounding and long-term wealth accumulation. Without a plan, we miss out on the potential benefits of investing early and consistently. Over time, this can significantly impact our ability to build wealth and achieve financial independence.

- **Difficulty in Achieving Dreams:** Planning for future financial goals aligns our actions and resources with our aspirations. Without a plan, our dreams may remain elusive or out of reach. Whether it's travelling, starting a business, or providing for our loved ones, inadequate financial planning can hinder our ability to turn these dreams into reality.

- **Lack of Control and Empowerment:** Planning for future financial goals empowers us to take control of our financial lives. Without a plan, we may feel overwhelmed, reactive, and dependent on external circumstances. This lack of control can lead to feelings of helplessness and hinder our ability to make meaningful progress towards our financial aspirations.

It's important to note that financial planning is a dynamic process, and goals may change over time. Regularly reviewing and adjusting our plans can help us adapt to evolving circumstances and maintain financial stability and growth. I recommend you do a review every 3 years. Generally in 3 year's time you have increased your salary, may be a job change, change of goals and aspirations, windfall gains in business or investment portfolio, this calls for a review.

In order to avoid these pitfalls, one can plan a few certain events that come to everyone's life:

1. Children's higher education fund

2. Marriage fund

3. Retirement Pension fund

4. Emergency Fund

Here's a tabular chart summarising the financial goals for an individual at 30

Financial Goal	Description
Building an Emergency Fund	Save 3 to 6 months' worth of living expenses in a separate account to cover unexpected expenses or income disruptions.
Paying Off Debt	Prioritise and develop a repayment plan to pay off high-interest debts, such as credit card debt, personal loans, or student loans.
Retirement Planning	Start contributing regularly to retirement accounts like Pension Plan, Provident Fund (PF), Public Provident Fund (PPF), or National Pension Scheme (NPS) for a comfortable retirement.

Financial Goal	Description
Saving for a Down Payment	Save towards a down payment for a home purchase or car. Research the property market and set a realistic savings target.
Investing for Wealth Accumulation	Explore investment options such as mutual funds, stocks, bonds, or real estate to grow wealth. Develop a diversified investment portfolio.
Education or Skill Development	Invest in education or skill development to enhance earning potential. Pursue further studies, attend professional courses, or acquire certifications or arrange funds for your Child's higher education.
Creating a Budget and Savings Plan	Establish a budget to track income and expenses. Allocate a certain percentage of income towards savings and investments.
Health and Insurance	Prioritise health and invest in health insurance coverage to protect against unexpected medical expenses.

Remember, these financial goals can be customised based on individual preferences and circumstances. It's important to review and adjust these goals as your financial situation evolves and seek guidance from a financial planner or adviser for personalised advice.

2.3   Design your Goals

Write down goals you want to achieve in the next 1 - 5 - 15 years.

Financial Goal	Description

* * *

What have we learned so far from Chapter 2:

4. ____

____

____

____

5. ____

____

____

____

6. ____

____

____

____

Note:

To deepen your understanding of the concepts covered in this chapter, please take the time to answer the following questions. Reflect on what you have learned and provide written responses to the open-ended questions. This exercise is designed to reinforce your knowledge and encourage you to apply the principles to your own financial planning.

What are my short-term goals? (0 - 5 years' timeline)

What are my long-term goals? (10 - 15 years' timeline)

What are some non-negotiable responsibilities I have which should be my financial goal?

Which goal should I address first? (Immediate and important)

Mention 5 things you want to achieve in the next year. (It can be a financial or personal goal)

Chapter 3

The Importance of Being Conscious about Money

Have you ever attended a dance class? Yes! It's that place where the dance teacher stands before you, passionately explaining how to move your body, counting rhythmically, "5, 6, 7, 8…" As you follow their instructions, something remarkable happens. You start to feel the rhythm, the flow, and the music in your bones. You begin to believe, "Yes, I am getting it," and that assumed truth becomes your reality.

Now, let's take a step away from the dance floor and onto the stage of financial awareness. Being money-conscious operates much like the dance class scenario. It's about understanding the rhythm of your finances, following a plan, and making your financial goals a reality.

Just as in a dance class, where you may start as a beginner and gradually become more proficient, becoming money-conscious involves a learning curve. It begins with understanding your financial situation, setting clear goals, and following a plan to achieve them. This process is akin to the dance teacher guiding your movements, counting out the steps, and helping you become a better dancer.

As you become more money-conscious, you begin to see your financial situation with clarity. You recognise where your money is going, how it's being spent, and how it can be better allocated to align with your goals. It's like learning a complex dance routine – at first, it may seem daunting, but with practice and dedication, it becomes second nature.

The "5, 6, 7, 8…" of financial consciousness involves budgeting, saving, investing, and managing debt. These are the steps that guide your financial dance. Each decision you make becomes a deliberate step toward financial security and success.

And just like in that dance class, when you confidently say, "Yes, I am getting it," in the realm of money, your beliefs shape your financial reality. When you believe in your ability to manage your finances wisely, you take control of your financial destiny. You make informed decisions that lead to financial stability and prosperity.

So, whether you're mastering a dance routine or mastering your finances, the process is remarkably similar. It's about becoming conscious of your actions, setting goals, and following a plan to achieve them. It's about believing in your ability to succeed and turning that belief into your financial reality.

So, are you ready to take the first step toward becoming money-conscious? Start counting your financial steps – "5, 6,

7, 8…" – and watch as your financial dance transforms into a symphony of success.

And so, just as a dancer perfects their moves through practice, you too can refine your financial steps and achieve your goals by becoming money-conscious. The rhythm of financial success is within your grasp.

Now, as we move forward in this financial journey, our next destination is creating a budget that works for you. Think of it as choreographing your financial dance – every income, expense, and financial goal has its place in the routine. Just like a well-executed dance performance, a carefully crafted budget can lead you to financial harmony and prosperity.

In the chapters that follow, I'll guide you through the process of creating a budget that aligns with your unique financial goals and lifestyle.

Financial consciousness is the state of being aware and mindful of one's financial situation. It encompasses a range of behaviours and attitudes that contribute to responsible money management. This awareness is not just about the numbers; it's about understanding the impact of financial decisions on overall well-being and life goals.

Once upon a time, in the bustling town of Rampur, there lived a wise old sage named Omkar. Omkar was not only the keeper of the community's wisdom but also a trusted adviser to many. His guidance was sought after by everyone, from the wealthiest businessmen to the humblest street vendors. One of the most important lessons Omkar taught was about the importance of being conscious about money and one's money habits.

In a quaint neighbourhood of Rampur, there was a young man named Rohan. Rohan was a talented artisan known for his exquisite, handcrafted jewellery. However, despite his talent, Rohan always found himself struggling financially. No matter how much he earned, his money seemed to disappear like water in the hot sun.

One day, feeling frustrated and hopeless, Rohan decided to seek advice from Omkar. He walked to the serene ashram where Omkar resided and asked for his wisdom.

"Omkar, I don't understand why I can never save any money," Rohan said. "I work hard and earn well, but it's gone before I know it. Can you help me?"

Omkar, with his kind eyes and deep understanding, nodded sagely. "Rohan, money is like a flowing river. If you don't channel it wisely, it will scatter and vanish. Let me tell you a story about 2 brothers who lived in this very town."

There were once 2 brothers, Suresh, and Rajesh. Their father left them an equal inheritance when he passed away. Suresh, the elder, was cautious and deliberate with his money. He made a budget, tracked his expenses, and saved a portion of his income each month. He invested in a small piece of land and started a modest shop, which gradually grew and prospered.

Rajesh, on the other hand, lived for the moment. He spent lavishly on parties, fine clothes, and expensive gadgets. He never kept track of his spending, always assuming that his inheritance would last forever. But soon enough, Rajesh found himself in debt, borrowing from friends and struggling to make ends meet.

Years passed, and while Suresh's shop flourished, Rajesh's financial woes only deepened. Eventually, Rajesh had no choice but to swallow his pride and ask his brother for help. Suresh welcomed him with open arms but also shared a crucial lesson.

"Rajesh," Suresh said, "the key to financial stability is not how much you have, but how you manage what you have. It's about being conscious of your spending, saving diligently, and investing wisely. Money, when respected, can grow, and provide security. When squandered, it disappears."

Rohan listened intently, absorbing the moral of the story. Omkar continued, "Rohan, your talent is your treasure. But to ensure it supports you, you must be mindful of your money. Create a budget, track your expenses, save regularly, and invest in your future. By developing good money habits, you can build a secure and prosperous life."

Inspired by Omkar's wisdom, Rohan went home and started implementing these principles. He made a budget, cut unnecessary expenses, and began saving a part of his income every month. Over time, Rohan not only managed to save money but also invested in better tools for his craft, leading to more business and higher earnings.

Years later, Rohan became one of the most successful artisans in Rampur, known not just for his skill but also for his financial acumen. Whenever someone asked him the secret of his success, he would smile and say, "It all started with a wise sage who taught me the importance of being conscious about my money and money habits."

3.1   Building a Conscious Budget

A conscious budget is not just a set of numbers; it's a reflection of your priorities and values. Creating a budget aligned with your financial goals involves identifying essential expenses, setting aside funds for savings, and allocating money for discretionary spending. Regularly tracking expenses ensures that your budget remains a dynamic and effective tool for financial consciousness.

Mindful Spending Habits

Conscious spending is a cornerstone of financial consciousness. It involves making intentional choices about where your money goes. This means distinguishing between needs and wants, recognising the value of purchases, and avoiding impulsive buying. Developing mindfulness in spending habits contributes significantly to maintaining financial health.

Saving with Purpose

Saving with purpose goes beyond merely stashing money away. It involves setting intentional savings goals, whether for emergencies, major purchases, or long-term investments. Automating savings and investments ensures consistency and helps you stay committed to your financial objectives.

Being Mindful of Debt

Financial consciousness extends to managing and minimising debt. It involves evaluating existing debts, making informed decisions about borrowing, and adopting strategies to avoid unnecessary debt. Being conscious of the impact of debt on your overall financial picture is key to maintaining a healthy financial stance.

Investing with Awareness

Investing with awareness requires ongoing financial education. Understanding different investment options, aligning investments with personal values and goals, and regularly reviewing investment portfolios contribute to a conscious and strategic approach to wealth-building.

3.2 The Emotional Aspect of Financial Consciousness

Recognising the emotional aspects of financial decisions is crucial. Understanding how emotions influence spending and saving habits enables individuals to make more rational and beneficial choices. Developing a healthy emotional relationship with money is an integral part of financial consciousness. How do you feel when money comes to you? It can be in the form of income you receive for the work you do. Do you feel happy and content, or do you feel lacking and less received? What is the feeling you get when you make payments or give money to people? Is it painful to let go of money? Do you feel you gave more than needed, do you feel sad or empty, or do you feel good when you are making the payments or when you pay to buy something? Your feelings decide your relationship with money. The relationship should be one of happiness, joy, and abundance. The feeling should be of contribution to the society and its people.

Teaching Financial Consciousness to Children

Early financial education sets the foundation for a lifetime of mindful money management. Parents can instil financial consciousness in children by introducing basic concepts, involving them in budgeting discussions, and encouraging responsible financial behaviours from an early age.

The Connection Between Health and Wealth

The link between financial consciousness and mental health is profound. Financial stress can adversely affect mental well-being, making it essential to prioritise a balanced and healthy financial mindset. Strategies such as setting realistic goals, practising self-compassion, and seeking support contribute to a positive financial outlook.

Practicing Gratitude in Finances

Cultivating gratitude in finances is a transformative practice. Acknowledging and appreciating what you have fosters contentment and reduces the temptation for excessive spending. Gratitude acts as a powerful antidote to the consumer-driven mindset, promoting financial consciousness.

Observe yourself whenever the next money goes out of your pocket - what do you feel? Make a note of it in various situations and when you are dealing with various people. Observe what you feel when money comes into your pocket. The amount can be big or small; the idea is to observe what you feel when money comes to you.

Give thanks for money when it comes to you. I appreciate the fact that you at least have the privilege to receive money and have the power to multiply it and grow. Gratitude attracts more money flow to you. It will help you multiply the money and also help you grow as an individual.

Have you read the book 'The Secret' by Rhonda Byrne? Unlocking the potential of gratitude, as outlined in 'The Secret,' can profoundly impact our financial journey. According to the book's teachings on the law of attraction, expressing gratitude for our existing financial state serves as a catalyst for attracting more abundance.

By acknowledging and appreciating the money we currently have, we send out positive vibrations to the universe, creating an environment conducive to receiving additional financial blessings.

"The Secret" emphasises a transformative shift in mindset from scarcity to abundance through the practice of gratitude. As we consistently express thanks for our financial well-being, we cultivate a wealth consciousness that aligns with the principles of the law of attraction.

This not only reduces stress associated with money matters but also positions us to recognise and seize new opportunities for financial growth. By making gratitude a daily practice, we not only enhance our current financial situation but also set in motion a powerful force that attracts more prosperity into our lives. In essence, by embracing the concept of gratitude, we leverage a tool that can positively shape our financial reality and lead us toward greater abundance.

* * *

What have we learned so far from Chapter 3:

4. ____

____

____

____

5. ____

____

____

____

6. ____

____

____

____

Note:

To deepen your understanding of the concepts covered in this chapter, please take the time to answer the following questions. Reflect on what you have learned and provide written responses to the open-ended questions. This exercise is designed to reinforce your knowledge and encourage you to apply the principles to your own financial planning.

Do I have a monthly budget that I stick to?

How much of my monthly income do I spend on shopping each month?

What percentage of my monthly income do I save?

Do I speak about money freely with my family?

Does my behaviour around money inspire my family to save and multiply money?

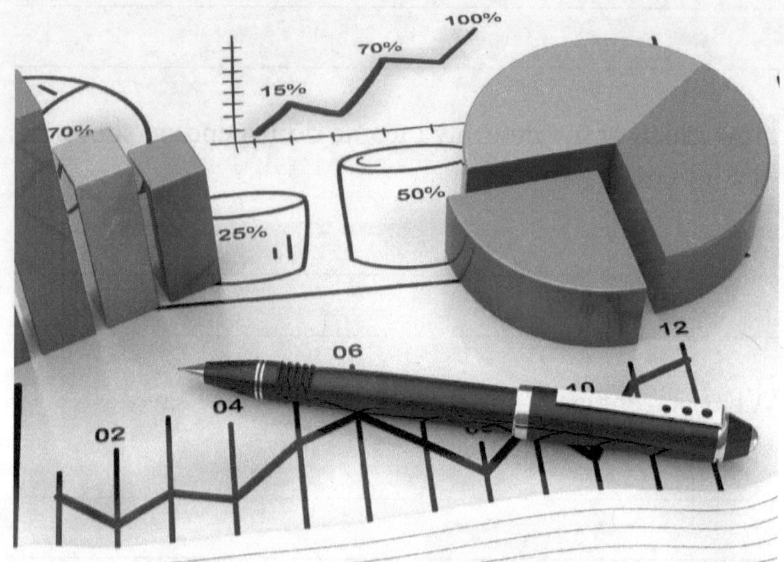

100%
70%
15%
50%
70%
25%
12
06
10
04
02

45

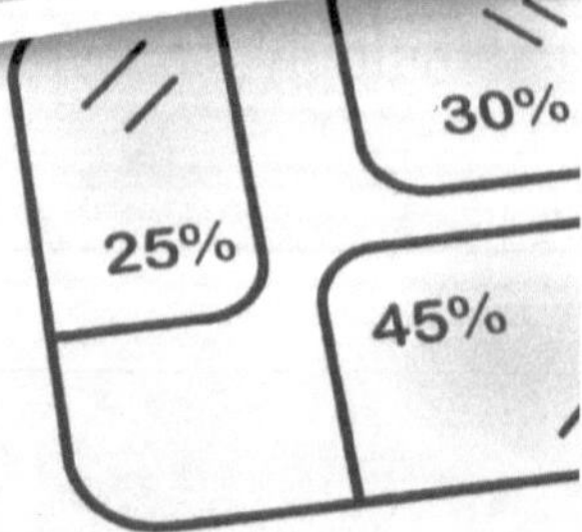

30%
25%
45%

Chapter 4

Creating a Budget That Works for You

Imagine you and your friends are planning an exciting road trip to Goa in December. To ensure that everyone has a great time and stays within their budget, you decide to make a road trip budget together.

First, you start by discussing the expenses you'll have during the trip. These may include fuel for the car, accommodation, food, activities, and any other miscellaneous expenses.

- **Fuel:** Estimate the distance to Goa and the average mileage of your car. Based on that, calculate the approximate fuel cost for the round trip. Let's say it comes to around Rs. 4,000.

- **Accommodation:** Research different types of accommodations available in Goa, such as hotels or guesthouses. Estimate the number of nights you'll be staying and the cost per night. For example, if you plan to stay for 3 nights and find a decent hotel for Rs. 2,000 per night, the total cost would be Rs. 6,000.

- **Food:** Discuss how you'll manage meals during the trip. You may decide to eat at local restaurants, try street food, or pack some snacks. Estimate an average amount for food expenses per day, keeping in mind that it might vary based on personal preferences. Let's say you allocate Rs. 500 per day for food, so for a five-day trip, it would be Rs. 2,500.

- **Activities:** Research the popular activities and attractions in Goa that you want to experience, such as water sports or sightseeing tours. Check the prices for each activity and allocate a budget accordingly. Let's say you plan to spend around Rs. 3,000 on activities.

- **Miscellaneous:** Set aside some money for unexpected expenses or souvenirs. It's good to have a buffer of around Rs. 1,000 to cover any unforeseen costs.

Once you have estimated the expenses for each category, add them up to calculate the total estimated cost of the trip. In this example, the estimated total would be Rs. 16,500 (Rs. 4,000 + Rs. 6,000 + Rs. 2,500 + Rs. 3,000 + Rs. 1,000).

Now, share the estimated cost with your friends and discuss how you can divide the expenses equally or based on individual preferences. It's important to consider everyone's budget limitations and find a fair way to split the costs.

Creating a budget for your road trip helps you stay organised and avoid overspending. It allows you to plan your finances in advance, make necessary adjustments, and ensure that everyone can enjoy the trip without any financial stress. During the trip, keep track of your expenses and compare them to your initial budget. This way, you can make adjustments as needed and stay within your planned spending limits.

Building upon the example of budgeting for a road trip to Goa, let's now explore the concept of personal financial budgeting. Personal financial budgeting involves managing your income and expenses to achieve your financial goals and ensure overall financial well-being. Here's how the concept applies:

4.1 Personal financial budget

- **Income Assessment:** Start by assessing your sources of income, such as your salary, freelance work, or any other earnings. Determine your total monthly or annual income. This will be the amount you have available to allocate towards your expenses and savings.

- **Fixed Expenses:** Identify your fixed expenses, which are recurring and relatively stable from month to month. These may include rent or mortgage payments, utility bills, loan repayments, insurance premiums, and subscriptions. Assign a specific amount to each fixed expense category based on your monthly obligations.

- **Variable Expenses:** Consider your variable expenses, which tend to fluctuate from month to month. These expenses can include groceries, dining out, transportation, entertainment, and clothing. Estimate an average amount for each category based on your spending patterns and allocate a budget accordingly.

- **Savings and Investments:** Determine how much you want to save or invest from your income. Set a target savings rate or a specific amount to allocate towards building an emergency fund, retirement savings, or other financial goals. Treat savings as a necessary expense and prioritise it in your budget.

- **Financial Goals:** Incorporate your financial goals into your budget. Whether it's saving for a down payment on a house, paying off debt, or planning a vacation, assign a portion of your income towards these goals. Be specific and realistic about the amounts and time frames needed to achieve them.

- **Review and Adjust:** Regularly review your budget to track your income, expenses, and progress towards your goals. Assess whether you're staying within your allocated amounts for each category. If necessary, make adjustments to ensure your budget aligns with your financial objectives and evolving circumstances.

- **Emergency Fund:** Include an emergency fund in your budget. Allocate a portion of your income towards building a safety net to cover unexpected expenses or income disruptions. Aim to save 3 to 6 months' worth of living expenses in this fund.

- **Monitoring and Discipline:** Monitor your expenses throughout the month, keeping track of every transaction. This helps you stay accountable and mindful of your spending habits. Use budgeting apps, spreadsheets, or expense-tracking tools to simplify the process.

- **Flexibility and Adaptation:** Be prepared to adjust your budget as needed. Life circumstances and financial priorities may change, requiring you to reallocate funds or revise your savings goals. Embrace flexibility and adaptability to ensure your budget remains effective.

By applying the concept of budgeting to personal finances, you gain better control over your money, make informed financial decisions, and work towards achieving your short-term and long-term goals. Remember, budgeting is a continuous process that requires regular evaluation, adjustments, and discipline. It empowers you to make intentional choices with your money and provides a roadmap to financial stability and success.

In the streets of New York City, a financial giant named Lehman Brothers once stood as a symbol of power and prestige. The year was 2008, and the global financial landscape was about to be shaken to its core.

Lehman Brothers was an investment bank with a rich history that was known for its involvement in major financial deals and transactions. Yet, behind the towering glass windows of its headquarters, a storm was brewing. The seeds of its downfall were sown in a series of decisions that ultimately led to one of the most catastrophic financial collapses in history.

At the heart of Lehman Brothers' failure was a combination of factors, including poor risk management, excessive risk-taking, and a failure to adapt to changing market dynamics. However, one of the key elements that played a pivotal role in its downfall was its neglect of effective budgeting practices for our understanding.

Lehman Brothers had been heavily involved in the subprime mortgage market, where loans were extended to individuals with risky credit profiles. These loans were packaged into mortgage-backed securities and sold to investors. As the housing bubble burst, the value of these securities plummeted, creating a domino effect across the financial system.

Despite early warning signs and mounting losses, Lehman Brothers continued to pour funds into these toxic assets.

The lack of accurate budgeting and risk assessment blinded the bank's leadership to the true extent of its exposure. They failed to accurately predict the potential losses that could arise from these investments.

As the financial crisis deepened, Lehman Brothers found itself grappling with a severe liquidity crisis. The bank's reliance on short-term borrowing and its inability to secure funding led to a dire situation. Without a well-structured budget that accounted for potential liquidity challenges, the bank was ill-prepared to weather the storm.

In September 2008, faced with mounting debts and dwindling investor confidence, Lehman Brothers filed for bankruptcy. The financial shockwaves reverberated around the world, triggering a global economic recession that affected millions of lives.

Lehman Brothers' downfall serves as a stark reminder of the importance of sound financial practices, including effective budgeting. Had the bank embraced rigorous budgeting techniques, accurately assessed risks, and prioritised risk management, its path might have been different. Budgeting could have provided the bank with the insights needed to diversify its investments, allocate resources strategically, and anticipate potential challenges.

The story of Lehman Brothers stands as a cautionary tale, reminding us that even the mightiest can fall if they lose sight of prudent financial management. In a world where economic uncertainties are a constant, the lessons from Lehman's collapse underscore the critical role that budgeting plays in maintaining stability, resilience, and long-term success.

The same is with individuals as it is with big corporations. Let's take the example of Ramesh and Sunita, a young couple living in Delhi.

Ramesh and Sunita were both working professionals in well-paying jobs. They enjoyed their lives to the fullest, dining at fancy restaurants, taking weekend trips, and indulging in expensive hobbies. Their income allowed them to maintain a comfortable lifestyle, and they rarely paid much attention to their spending habits.

As the years went by, Ramesh and Sunita's financial situation took an unexpected turn. They decided to start a family, and soon, they were blessed with twins. With the addition of their children, their expenses naturally increased. However, they continued spending without much consideration for their changing financial dynamics.

Despite their seemingly good incomes, Ramesh and Sunita found themselves struggling to meet their growing expenses. They often relied on credit cards to cover their lifestyle choices, thinking that their high incomes would always bail them out. Their failure to budget and monitor their expenses left them with mounting credit card debt and little savings.

The turning point came when Ramesh faced a job loss due to a company restructuring. Suddenly, their household was down to a single income, and their lack of budgeting became painfully evident. They were unable to keep up with their lifestyle expenses, debt repayments, and children's needs, all on a single income.

Their situation worsened as they were forced to dip into their savings, leaving them vulnerable in case of emergencies. Ramesh and Sunita realised the importance of budgeting the hard way, as they were faced with the harsh reality of financial instability.

Their story serves as a lesson on the significance of budgeting. While their initial high incomes gave them a false sense of financial security, it was their lack of financial planning and budgeting that led them to a difficult situation. Their experience underscores the importance of living within one's means, tracking expenses, and building a strong financial foundation to weather unexpected challenges.

Ramesh and Sunita's story shows that effective budgeting is not just about managing day-to-day expenses; it's about preparing for the uncertainties that life can bring. By creating a well-structured budget and being mindful of their spending, individuals can better navigate financial ups and downs and secure their financial futures.

4.2   Format to create a personal finance budget

In this table, you can start by filling in the different expense categories under "Fixed Expenses" and "Variable Expenses." Estimate how much you want to allocate for each category in the "Monthly Budget" column.

As the month progresses, track your actual expenses under the "Actual Expenses" column. You can refer to your bank statements, receipts, or expense-tracking apps to record the actual amounts spent in each category.

To calculate the "Difference," subtract the actual expenses from the monthly budget for each category. A positive difference indicates that you stayed within your budget, while a negative difference indicates that you exceeded your budget. Finally, at the bottom, calculate the total income, total expenses, and savings by summing up the corresponding amounts.

This tabular form will help you track and compare your planned budget with your actual expenses, providing insights into areas where you may need to adjust or control your spending. It serves as a visual tool to evaluate your progress, make informed financial decisions, and work towards achieving your financial goals. Feel free to customise the table based on your specific expense categories and goals. You can add or modify rows as needed to reflect your unique financial situation.

Here's a simple tabular form that can help you start your journey of budgeting:

Expense Category	Monthly Budget	Actual Expenses	Difference
Fixed Expenses			
Rent/Mortgage			
Utilities			
Loan Repayments			
Insurance Premiums			
Subscriptions			
Variable Expenses			
Groceries			
Dining Out			
Transportation			
Entertainment			
Clothing			
Savings and Investments			
Emergency Fund			
Retirement Savings			
Other Financial Goals			
Total Income			
Total Expenses			
Savings			

* * *

What have we learned so far from Chapter 4:

10. ____

____

____

____

11. ____

____

____

____

12. ____

____

____

____

Note:

To deepen your understanding of the concepts covered in this chapter, please take the time to answer the following questions. Reflect on what you have learned and provide written responses to the open-ended questions. This exercise is designed to reinforce your knowledge and encourage you to apply the principles to your own financial planning.

Do I now have clarity on my fixed expenses?

Do I now have clarity on my variable expense?

Do I now have clarity on my future monthly expenses?

Do I now have clarity on the money that I am overspending on?

Do I feel I have enough or less money flow every month?

MONEY
MANAGEMENT

Chapter 5

Managing Debt and Credit Wisely

Maya was a dedicated and passionate school teacher who loved her job. She was always committed to providing the best education for her students. However, Maya had one challenge that was causing her financial stress – credit card debt.

Maya loved the convenience of her credit card and often used it for everyday expenses. She would swipe her card without much thought, thinking she could pay off the balance later. Over time, her credit card debt began to accumulate, and she found it increasingly difficult to keep up with the payments.

One day, Maya realised that her credit card debt was taking a toll on her financial well-being. She felt overwhelmed and worried about how she would manage to pay off the mounting balances. That's when she decided it was time to take control of her finances and learn how to manage her debt wisely.

Maya started by assessing her overall financial situation. She gathered all her credit card statements and listed the outstanding balances and interest rates for each card. This helped her get a clear picture of her debt and the impact it was having on her finances.

Next, Maya researched strategies for managing credit card debt. She learned about the importance of making more than just the minimum payments and prioritising high-interest debts. With this newfound knowledge, Maya developed a debt repayment plan. Maya's plan involved creating a budget that allowed her to allocate extra money towards her credit card payments. She made a commitment to reduce her discretionary spending and cut back on non-essential expenses. By doing so, she could free up more money to put towards paying off her debt.

Maya also reached out to her credit card companies to negotiate lower interest rates. With some persistence and explaining her financial situation, she was able to secure reduced interest rates, which helped her pay off her debt more efficiently.

As Maya followed her debt repayment plan, she realised the importance of using credit wisely. She learned to avoid unnecessary credit card usage and to only charge what she could afford to pay off in full each month. Maya understood that credit cards were a tool, and when used responsibly, they could be beneficial.

Over time, Maya's dedication and disciplined approach paid off. She successfully paid off her credit card debt, one balance at a time. It was a journey that required sacrifice and commitment, but Maya emerged stronger and more financially empowered.

Through her experience, Maya learned valuable lessons about managing debt and credit wisely. She discovered the importance of budgeting, living within her means, and being mindful of her spending habits. Maya became an advocate for financial literacy, sharing her story with her colleagues and students to inspire them to make informed financial decisions.

In India, credit card companies typically charge interest on the outstanding balance if the full payment is not made by the due date. Here are the details of how credit card interest works and why it can be a costly affair if the debt is not paid on time. Before that lets understand some terms used by credit card companies.

- **Annual Percentage Rate (APR):** Credit card companies specify an Annual Percentage Rate (APR), which represents the interest rate charged on the outstanding balance. The APR is usually expressed as a percentage per annum.

- **Billing Cycle and Statement Date:** Credit card statements are generated at the end of each billing cycle, which is typically a 30-day period. The statement date marks the end of the billing cycle.

- **Grace Period:** Credit cards usually offer a grace period, which is the period between the statement date and the payment due date. During the grace period, interest is not charged on new purchases if the previous statement's outstanding balance is paid in full.

- **Minimum Amount Due:** The credit card statement specifies a Minimum Amount Due, which is the minimum payment required to be made by the due date to avoid late payment charges. However, paying only the minimum amount due will result in interest charges on the remaining balance.

- **Interest Calculation:** If the full outstanding balance is not paid by the due date, interest is calculated on the remaining balance. The interest is usually calculated daily or monthly based on the average daily balance method.

- **High-Interest Rates:** Credit card interest rates in India can be relatively high, often ranging from 24% to 48% per annum. These high rates make it crucial to pay off credit card debt promptly to avoid accumulating significant interest charges.

- **Compound Interest:** Credit card interest is often compounded, which means that interest is charged not only on the principal balance but also on any accrued interest from previous billing cycles. This compounding effect can significantly increase the overall interest cost over time.

- **Costly Debt Accumulation:** If credit card debt is not paid on time and continues to accumulate, the interest charges can quickly add up, making it challenging to repay the debt. The longer the debt remains unpaid, the more costly it becomes due to the compounding effect of interest.

- **Late Payment Charges:** In addition to interest charges, credit card companies also impose late payment fees if the minimum amount due or the full outstanding balance is not paid by the due date. These charges further increase the overall cost of carrying credit card debt.

It's essential to understand the terms and conditions of your credit card agreement, including the interest rates, billing cycle, grace period, and payment due dates. By paying off the full outstanding balance within the grace period, you can avoid interest charges altogether.

However, if you cannot pay the full amount, it is advisable to pay as much as possible above the minimum amount to reduce the interest cost. It's important to be diligent in managing credit card debt, as carrying a balance and accumulating interest can lead to a cycle of debt that becomes increasingly difficult to overcome.

Remember, responsible credit card usage involves paying off the outstanding balance on time and using credit cards as a convenient payment tool rather than a means of borrowing long-term debt.

5.1 Paying debt in time vs taking your own time

Here are 2 examples in tabular form to help you understand the impact of paying credit card debt on time versus making only minimum payments for 12 months:

Example 1: Paying Credit Card Debt on Time

Month	Starting Balance	Payment	Interest Charged	Ending Balance
Month 1	₹ 10,000	₹ 10,000	₹ 0	₹ 0
Month 2	-	-	-	-
Month 3	-	-	-	-
Month 4	-	-	-	-
Month 5	-	-	-	-
Month 6	-	-	-	-
Month 7	-	-	-	-
Month 8	-	-	-	-
Month 9	-	-	-	-
Month 10	-	-	-	-
Month 11	-	-	-	-
Month 12	-	-	-	-

In this example, by paying off the full outstanding balance of ₹10,000 on time each month, no interest is charged, and the balance is reduced to zero within 12 months.

Example 2: Making Minimum Payments for 12 Months (36% Interest Rate)

Month	Starting Balance	Payment	Interest Charged	Ending Balance
Month 1	₹ 10,000	₹ 500	₹ 300	₹ 9,800
Month 2	₹ 9,800	₹ 500	₹ 294	₹ 9,594
Month 3	₹ 9,594	₹ 500	₹ 287	₹ 9,381
Month 4	₹ 9,381	₹ 500	₹ 281	₹ 9,162
Month 5	₹ 9,162	₹ 500	₹ 275	₹ 8,937
Month 6	₹ 8,937	₹ 500	₹ 268	₹ 8,705
Month 7	₹ 8,705	₹ 500	₹ 261	₹ 8,466
Month 8	₹ 8,466	₹ 500	₹ 254	₹ 8,220
Month 9	₹ 8,220	₹ 500	₹ 247	₹ 7,967
Month 10	₹ 7,967	₹ 500	₹ 239	₹ 7,706
Month 11	₹ 7,706	₹ 500	₹ 231	₹ 7,437
Month 12	₹ 7,437	₹ 500	₹ 224	₹ 7,161

In this updated example, we consider a 36% annual interest rate (3% per month). The interest charged each month is calculated based on the outstanding balance multiplied by the monthly interest rate.

Please note that a 36% interest rate is relatively high, and it highlights the importance of paying off credit card debt as soon as possible to avoid accumulating significant interest charges. It's always advisable to review the specific terms and conditions of your credit card agreement to understand the interest rates and payment terms that apply to your situation.

But there is also this concept of good debt and bad debt.

5.2   Good Debt and Bad Debt

In the vibrant city of Mumbai, there lived a wise old man named Mr. Patel, who was renowned for his knowledge of personal finance. Mr. Patel resided in a cosy apartment in the bustling Dadar area, where people from all around would come to seek his sage advice.

One bright morning, a young woman named Riya knocked on Mr. Patel's door, her heart fluttering with excitement and confusion. Riya had just received her first credit card and was eager to use it, but she had heard many warnings about the perils of debt. She hoped Mr. Patel could help her understand the difference between good debt and bad debt.

Mr. Patel welcomed Riya with a warm smile and offered her a seat at his dining table. "Ah, Riya, you have come with a very important question. Let me tell you a story that might help you understand."

"Once, in a nearby neighbourhood, there were 2 best friends: Sameer and Neha. Both wanted to buy their own homes. Sameer decided to take out a loan to purchase a flat in an up-and-coming area. He planned carefully, ensuring he had a steady income to pay off his loan while his property appreciated in value. This Riya is what we call 'good debt.' Sameer used his loan to invest in something that would grow in value and ultimately increase his wealth."

Riya's eyes sparkled with interest as she listened.

"Neha, on the other hand," Mr. Patel continued, "decided to use her loan to go on an extravagant vacation. She travelled to exotic destinations and had a wonderful time, but soon, the credit card bills started piling up. Neha found herself drowning in debt with nothing to show for it but memories. This is 'bad debt,' Riya. Neha's debt did not help her grow her wealth; instead, it drained her resources."

Mr. Patel paused to let the story sink in. "So you see, Riya, the key difference lies in how the debt is used. Good debt is an investment in your future—it could be a home loan, an education loan, or even a business loan, as long as it helps you build wealth or improve your financial situation. Bad debt, on the other hand, is for things that do not provide a return, like luxury vacations or excessive shopping. Always ask yourself if the debt you're taking on will help you grow or hold you back."

Riya nodded thoughtfully. "Thank you, Mr. Patel. I understand now. I'll be careful with my credit card and use it wisely."

"That's the spirit, Riya," said Mr. Patel, beaming with pride. "Remember, the choices you make today will shape your financial future. Choose wisely, and prosperity will follow."

The difference between good debt and bad debt lies in the nature of the debt and the potential long-term benefits or drawbacks it offers. Here's an explanation of each:

- **Good Debt:** Good debt refers to borrowing money for investments or assets that have the potential to increase in value over time or generate long-term benefits. Here are some characteristics of good debt:

    a. **Investment Purpose:** Good debt is often associated with investments that have the potential to appreciate or generate income. For example, taking a mortgage to purchase a home or obtaining a student loan to finance education can be considered good debts.

b. **Positive Return on Investment:** Good debt has the potential to provide a positive return on investment. For instance, investing in a business or acquiring real estate properties that generate rental income can be considered good debts if the returns outweigh the borrowing costs.

c. **Enhances Financial Well-being:** Good debt can contribute to improving your financial situation in the long run. For example, student loans may lead to better career opportunities and higher income potential, ultimately benefiting your financial well-being.

d. **Low Interest Rates:** Good debt often comes with relatively low interest rates, making it more affordable over time. This is especially true for loans taken for assets like homes or education, as they tend to have favourable interest rates compared to high-interest credit card debt.

e. **Potential Tax Advantages:** Some forms of good debt, such as mortgage loans, may offer tax benefits. For instance, mortgage interest payments may be tax-deductible, reducing the overall cost of borrowing.

- **Bad Debt:** Bad debt refers to borrowing for items that depreciate in value or do not provide any long-term benefits. Bad debts typically have the following characteristics:

  a. **Consumer Goods:** Bad debt often arises from financing unnecessary or luxury consumer goods, such as high-end electronics, luxury vehicles, or expensive vacations. These items typically lose value quickly and do not contribute to long-term financial well-being.

  b. **High-Interest Rates:** Bad debt tends to have high-interest rates, especially when obtained through credit cards or personal loans. These high rates can result in substantial interest charges, making it challenging to pay off the debt efficiently.

  c. **No Return on Investment:** Bad debt does not offer any potential for generating income or appreciating in value. Instead, it represents expenditures that provide short-term satisfaction without contributing to long-term financial stability or growth.

  d. **Risk of Overextending Finances:** Accumulating too much bad debt can lead to financial strain and difficulty in meeting repayment obligations. It can negatively impact your credit score and limit your ability to secure favourable borrowing terms in the future.

  e. **Emotional and Impulsive Spending:** Bad debt often results from impulsive or emotional spending decisions, where individuals may not consider the long-term financial consequences of their purchases.

Differentiating between good debt and bad debt can help individuals make informed financial decisions. While good debt can contribute to wealth-building and financial progress, it's important to exercise caution and avoid excessive borrowing or falling into the trap of bad debts that hinder financial stability.

Remember, managing debt wisely involves considering the purpose, potential returns, interest rates, and long-term benefits of the debt. Striving to minimise bad debts and prioritise good debts can lead to a more secure financial future.

Here's a tabular chart to help you identify if an investment can be categorised as good debt or bad debt:

Criteria	Good Debt	Bad Debt
Purpose	Investments with potential for appreciation or income generation, such as real estate, business ventures, or education	Financing consumer goods or unnecessary luxury items
Return on Investment	Potential for positive returns or increased income over time	No potential for returns or income generation
Long-term Benefits	Enhances financial well-being and contributes to long-term stability or growth.	Provides short-term satisfaction without long-term benefits
Interest Rates	Often have lower interest rates, making them more affordable over time	Tend to have higher interest rates, resulting in substantial interest charges
Tax Advantages	Some investments offer tax benefits, such as mortgage interest deductions	No tax advantages associated with the investment
Risk Assessment	Considered relatively low-risk or manageable risks with potential for rewards	Higher risk or no potential for significant rewards

Please note that this chart provides a general overview and should be used as a starting point for evaluating investments only. Many have this question about if I have to buy a house property and is it wise to buy one and how much can I afford to pay as EMI.

Once upon a time, in bustling Bangalore, a young IT professional named Kiran lived there. He had always dreamt of owning his own house, a place he could call his own sanctuary. After years of hard work and saving, Kiran finally found the perfect property, a cosy apartment in a vibrant neighbourhood.

Filled with excitement, Kiran decided to take a home loan to make his dream of homeownership come true. The bank approved his loan application, and Kiran signed the dotted line, eagerly anticipating a life in his new home.

However, what Kiran didn't realise at the time was that his monthly EMI (Equated Monthly Instalment) was quite high in proportion to his monthly income. Eager to own a property and caught up in the thrill of fulfilling his dream, Kiran hadn't carefully considered the impact of such a significant financial commitment.

As months went by, Kiran started to feel the burden of the hefty EMI. It consumed more than 30% of his monthly income, leaving him with limited funds to cover other essential expenses. With a substantial portion of his salary dedicated to the EMI, Kiran found it challenging to maintain a comfortable lifestyle and save for unforeseen circumstances.

The strain of managing the EMI payment affected Kiran's overall financial well-being. He had to cut back on social activities, dining out, and even postponed plans for further skill development. The stress of meeting his monthly financial obligations weighed heavily on Kiran's mind, affecting his work and personal life.

Realising the gravity of the situation, Kiran sought advice from a financial adviser. The adviser emphasised the importance of maintaining a healthy balance between his EMI and monthly income. He advised Kiran to ensure that the EMI falls between 25% to 35% of his monthly income. He also warned against buying a property simply because everyone else was doing it or being lured by fancy properties that stretched his budget.

The financial adviser encouraged Kiran to differentiate between his needs and wants. He asked Kiran to question himself if the property was a genuine need or simply a want. If it was a want, the adviser advised Kiran to evaluate whether he could postpone the purchase and arrange for additional funds to avoid a financial crunch.

Moreover, the adviser stressed the importance of the thumb rule - not exceeding 30% of his salary on the EMI per person in the family. Following this rule would give Kiran the financial bandwidth to grow better and live comfortably.

The financial adviser also cautioned Kiran against the misconception that owning a high-value asset at a young age equates to success. He explained that such a move could lead to liquidity issues and hinder Kiran's ability to handle unexpected financial situations.

"Success and financial freedom," the adviser said, "is not just about owning expensive assets or living in a fancy apartment. True success is when you have money in your pocket and financial security for the future."

The adviser emphasised the importance of maintaining a healthy balance between his EMI and monthly income. He recommended exploring options to refinance the loan or negotiate with the bank to lower the EMI amount.

Kiran decided to take action and renegotiate his loan terms with the bank. He knew that if negotiation was not in his favour, he would have to sell the house and buy something that fit his budget and pocket. Fortunately, the negotiating bank extended the loan tenure, increasing it from 20 years to 30 years, reducing the EMI amount; Kiran felt relieved as it eased his financial burden significantly. He also took steps to increase his income through upskilling and exploring freelance opportunities, which gave him more financial breathing room. Though he will end up paying more for the same house in interest for 10 more years, he is foresighted in paying one extra EMI every year to reduce the debt burden.

With time, Kiran managed to strike a better balance between his EMI and income. The reduced financial strain allowed him to enjoy his new home, invest in himself, and achieve a better-quality of life.

If you have this as a question for you, start filling in the blanks and find out for yourself!

5.3 Should I Buy a Second Property? – Financial Evaluation Worksheet

Step 1: Assess Your Financial Situation

Monthly Income (after taxes): _________________

Monthly Expenses (including rent, utilities, groceries, etc.):

____

Total Savings and Investments: _________________

Outstanding   Debts   (credit   cards,   loans,   etc.):

____

Step 2: Determine EMI Affordability

Calculate 30% of your Monthly Income:

30% of Monthly Income = 30% x Monthly Income

Calculate EMI Affordability:

EMI Affordability = 30% of Monthly Income – Monthly Expenses (EMI you already have)

Step 3: Assess Additional Costs

Down Payment:

Consider the down payment required for the property. Ensure you have enough savings set aside for this.

Property Registration and Legal Fees:

Estimate the additional costs involved in registering the property and any legal fees.

Maintenance and Utility Costs:

Factor in ongoing maintenance and utility costs associated with homeownership.

Step 4: Calculate Total Budget

Total Budget = Total Savings and Investments + EMI Affordability + Down Payment

Step 5: Determine Loan Eligibility

Contact lenders or banks to understand your eligibility for a home loan based on your financial situation.

Calculate Loan Eligibility:

Loan Eligibility = Lender's Maximum Loan to Value (LTV) Ratio x Total Budget

Step 6: Assess Your Decision

Based on your Total Budget and Loan Eligibility, assess if it aligns with the property you desire to purchase.

Consider the long-term impact of the EMI on your monthly cash flow and lifestyle.

Step 7: Seek Professional Advice

Consult a financial adviser to discuss your financial goals, analyse your financial situation, and get personalised advice on homeownership. Review the worksheet with the financial adviser to ensure a well-informed decision.

Remember, buying a property is a significant financial commitment, and it's crucial to thoroughly evaluate your financial readiness and consider both short-term and long-term implications. This worksheet can help you make an informed decision and ensure that buying a property fits well within your financial capacity and goals.

* * *

What have we learned so far from chapter 5:

13. ____

____

____

____

14. ____

____

____

____

15. ____

____

____

____

Note:

To deepen your understanding of the concepts covered in this chapter, please take the time to answer the following questions. Reflect on what you have learned and provide written responses to the open-ended questions. This exercise is designed to reinforce your knowledge and encourage you to apply the principles to your own financial planning.

What percentage of my monthly income goes into EMI? If it exceeds the thumb rule, what steps can I take to reduce my debt burden?

Do I now have clarity on my credit card expenses?

Do I need to use a credit card for things I could buy upfront to reduce credit card debt?

Do I now have a plan to clear my credit card debt?

Do I need to have more than one credit card, and why?

Chapter 6

Investing for the Future

Before we understand what investing for the future means we need to understand what financial forecasting is, we must take a look at Maslow's Hierarchy of Needs.

6.1   Maslow's Hierarchy of Needs

Developed by psychologist Abraham Maslow in the mid-20th century, Maslow's Hierarchy of Needs is a psychological theory that outlines the 5 levels of human needs arranged in a pyramid. The theory suggests that individuals are motivated to fulfil lower-level needs before moving on to higher level ones.

- **Physiological Needs**: At the base of the pyramid are physiological needs, such as food, water, shelter, and clothing. These basic requirements must be met for survival and form the foundation of human motivation.

- **Safety Needs**: The next level encompasses safety needs, including personal security, health, and financial stability. Once physiological needs are reasonably satisfied, individuals seek safety and protection from physical and economic threats.

- **Love and Belongingness**: This level represents social needs, such as the desire for love, friendship, and a sense of belonging to a community or family.

- **Esteem Needs**: The fourth level involves esteem needs, which include self-esteem and the need for recognition, respect, and achievement. Individuals strive for a positive self-image and seek recognition from others.

- **Self-Actualisation**: At the top of the pyramid is self-actualisation, representing the desire for personal growth, fulfilment, and reaching one's full potential.

The Financial Learnings from Maslow's Hierarchy of Needs

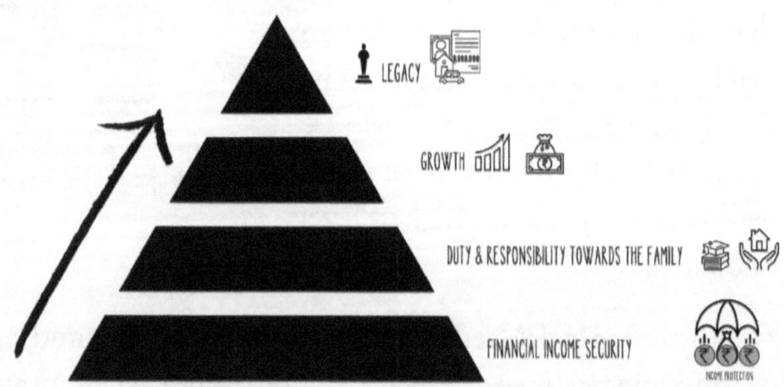

Aligning Maslow's Hierarchy of Needs with a financial pyramid provides a nuanced perspective on the psychological and financial dimensions of personal development. At the base of the financial pyramid, Maslow's safety needs are mirrored, and these are the foundational elements related to financial security and stability. This encompasses essentials such as a secure income, emergency fund, and insurance, addressing the fundamental need for economic safety.

Moving up the financial pyramid, the second level correlates with Maslow's concept of duty and responsibility. Here, financial goals expand to include obligations such as debt repayment, family support, and meeting basic lifestyle needs. This level reflects the financial responsibility individuals undertake to fulfil their societal and familial duties, mirroring Maslow's emphasis on social and esteem needs.

The third level of the financial pyramid corresponds to Maslow's aspirations, encompassing personal and professional growth. Financial goals at this stage involve investments in education, skill development, and career advancement. This level aligns with Maslow's idea of self-actualisation, as individuals strive to achieve their highest potential and pursue fulfilling aspirations.

As we ascend the financial pyramid, reaching the higher levels, parallels emerge with Maslow's self-transcendence stage. Contribution and legacy become the focal points, mirroring Maslow's emphasis on altruism and making a meaningful impact beyond oneself. Financial goals at this pinnacle involve philanthropy, legacy planning, and contributing to community or societal betterment.

In this synthesis of Maslow's Hierarchy of Needs and the financial pyramid, we recognise that financial well-being is intricately connected to our psychological needs and personal development. By understanding the interplay between basic safety, duty, aspirations, and the pursuit of contribution and legacy, individuals can create a comprehensive financial plan that not only secures their immediate needs but also fosters holistic personal growth and societal impact.

6.2 Financial Forecasting

Financial forecasting in personal financial planning involves projecting future financial outcomes based on current financial data, economic trends, and individual financial goals. It's a strategic process that uses past and present financial information to make informed predictions about future financial situations. By connecting the financial learnings from Maslow's Hierarchy of Needs to financial forecasting, individuals can create a more comprehensive and holistic approach to managing their finances.

Importance of Financial Forecasting:

Financial forecasting serves as the cornerstone for building a secure financial future. It allows individuals to anticipate and plan for their financial needs across various life stages, from securing the basics to fulfilling responsibilities and aspirations, and contributing to broader goals.

Consequences of Neglecting Financial Forecasting:

Failure to engage in financial forecasting can lead to a haphazard approach to money management. Without a clear plan, individuals may find themselves unprepared for unexpected expenses, unable to meet duties and responsibilities, and falling short of achieving their aspirations. Moreover, overlooking the higher tiers of financial planning may result in missed opportunities for contribution and legacy building.

Benefits of Financial Forecasting:

- **Security and Stability:** Financial forecasting ensures a stable foundation by addressing basic needs and establishing a safety net for unforeseen circumstances.

- **Strategic Decision-Making:** With a clear financial forecast, individuals can make informed decisions about investments, education, and career choices, aligning their financial strategies with personal aspirations.

- **Fulfilment of Responsibilities:** Financial forecasting facilitates the fulfilment of duties and responsibilities, fostering a sense of accomplishment and social contribution.

- **Holistic Growth:** By encompassing aspirations in the financial plan, individuals can strive for self-actualisation, continuously improving and evolving personally and professionally.

- **Legacy and Contribution:** Engaging in long-term financial forecasting allows for the intentional creation of a legacy, be it through philanthropy, community contributions, or other impactful ventures.

Creating a Richer and More Fulfilled Life:

Financial forecasting becomes a powerful tool in creating a richer and more fulfilled life when coupled with intentional planning and action. By understanding the stages of financial well-being and aligning goals with Maslow's hierarchy, individuals can achieve a holistic and purpose-driven financial life.

Through strategic financial planning, individuals not only secure their own needs but also contribute positively to society. As financial goals extend beyond personal gain to include responsibility, aspiration fulfilment, and legacy creation, a sense of fulfilment emerges. Taking deliberate steps towards financial goals, guided by a well-thought-out forecast, provides a roadmap to a richer and more purposeful life, where one's financial success is intertwined with personal growth and societal impact.

Let's navigate the financial landscape with Sam, a 30-year-old family man residing in India with his wife and 2 daughters (aged 5 and 1), faces unique considerations in his financial forecasting. Aligning with Maslow's Hierarchy of Needs, Sam's plan prioritises the well-being and future of his family.

Safety and Stability (Base of the Financial Pyramid):

- **Emergency Fund:** Establishing a robust emergency fund is essential, covering at least 6 months of living expenses. Sam may consider holding this fund in a savings account or Fixed Deposits for accessibility.

- **Insurance:** In India, health insurance is paramount. Sam should invest in comprehensive health coverage equal to 5 times his annual income for his family. Additionally, life insurance policies can provide financial stability in the event of unforeseen circumstances. Generally, term insurance should be at least 10 times the annual income. This will help secure the income coming into the house.

Duty and Responsibility (Second Level):

- **Debt Repayment:** If Sam has any outstanding loans, such as a home loan or personal loan, a portion of his financial plan should be allocated to debt repayment.

- **Children's Education Fund:** India offers education-specific savings plans, like an insurance policy or Sukanya Samriddhi Yojana, which Sam can leverage for his daughter's education. Considering he has 2 daughters, the overall expenses will be high for his age of 50 - 60 as both daughters are also going to need funds one after the other. An assured returns plan for their education from the age of 18 - 23 years will give them peace of mind and assurance of their education. Combining equity investment with an extra layer of support is always a good idea.

Aspirations (Third Level):

- **Real Estate Investment:** Given the cultural significance of homeownership in India, Sam may aspire to own a home. Allocating funds towards real estate or exploring home loan options could be part of his financial plan. This accumulation of money can be done in a systematic format with the help of SIP in Mutual funds. Or directly investing in stocks.

- **Investments:** Sam can consider investing in Indian financial instruments, such as mutual funds, the Public Provident Fund (PPF), or the National Pension System (NPS), to align with his aspirations for financial growth.

Contribution and Legacy (Top of the Financial Pyramid):

- **Life Insurance for Legacy Planning:** In India, life insurance can serve dual purposes – providing financial protection and acting as an investment tool. Sam may explore traditional life insurance plans or Term Insurance Plans for legacy planning. Adding an annuity scheme will help him design his retirement effectively.

- **Estate Planning:** Creating a will is crucial in India to ensure a smooth transfer of assets. Sam may also explore options like family trusts for effective estate planning. This can be done by appointing a good lawyer. Creating a cash flow mechanism using Insurance money to create a steady flow of income is an advanced plan used by industrialists to keep their estates running.

6.3   Use of Financial Tools

Financial Tools for Sam in India:

- **Family Health Insurance:** Explore family health insurance policies offered by reputable insurers in India.

- **PPF and Sukanya Samriddhi Yojana:** Leverage these government-backed savings schemes for long-term goals like children's education and marriage.

- **Life Insurance Policies:** They will help him with guaranteed cash flow requirements for a child's higher education and marriage, and they will also be a good cash flow tool for retirement. The investment done in insurance is also tax effective and has double tax saving benefits like Sec 80c and Sec 1010D.

- **Mutual Funds:** Diversify investments through SIPs (Systematic Investment Plans) in mutual funds based on risk appetite and financial goals.

Investing in the stock market as a pure equity investment can help him create a huge corpus for his future.

By tailoring his financial forecast to the Indian context and leveraging these tools, Sam can strategically navigate the financial landscape. This approach ensures that his family's present needs are met while creating a foundation for a secure and prosperous future in India.

6.4 Cost of Not Planning

If Sam fails to engage in comprehensive financial planning, several potential consequences may arise, impacting both his immediate and long-term financial well-being:

- **Financial Instability:** Without a solid financial plan, Sam may face increased vulnerability to financial shocks. Unexpected expenses, emergencies, or economic downturns could disrupt the family's financial stability, making it challenging to meet day-to-day needs.

- **Inadequate Protection:** Lack of appropriate insurance coverage, especially health and life insurance, may expose Sam and his family to significant financial risks. In the event of unforeseen medical expenses or a loss of income, the absence of adequate insurance could lead to financial strain or completely erode his savings and investments.

- **Missed Investment Opportunities:** Failing to strategically invest in Indian financial instruments might result in missed opportunities for wealth accumulation and growth. Sam may not harness the potential returns offered by instruments like mutual funds, stocks, PPF, or other investment avenues, hampering the family's ability to build wealth over time.

- **Limited Education Funding:** Neglecting to set up dedicated funds for his daughter's education, such as utilising schemes like Sukanya Samriddhi Yojana, SIP or Child education policies, may hinder their access to quality education. This oversight could limit their future opportunities and potential career paths.

- **Delayed Homeownership:** If Sam's aspiration is to own a home, the lack of financial planning may lead to delays in realising this goal. Without a clear strategy and savings plan, homeownership may remain elusive, impacting the family's sense of stability and accomplishment.

- **Ineffective Legacy Planning:** Without adequate life insurance coverage and estate planning, Sam may compromise the financial security of his family in the long-term. The absence of a well-structured legacy plan could result in legal complexities and financial uncertainties for his loved ones in the event of unforeseen circumstances.

- **Missed Tax Optimisation:** Failing to integrate tax-efficient strategies into his financial plan may lead to missed opportunities for tax savings. Sam could overlook potential deductions and exemptions, resulting in higher tax liabilities.

- **Retirement Insecurity:** Inadequate contributions to retirement accounts like the National Pension System (NPS) or Annuity policies may leave Sam and his wife financially unprepared for their post-employment years. This oversight could impact their ability to maintain their desired lifestyle and cover healthcare expenses in retirement.

6.5 Your Plan of Action

Create a table outlining a plan of action for you based on the financial considerations and potential consequences mentioned above:

Financial Aspect	Action Steps for Sam	Tools/Strategies
Safety and Stability	Establish a 6-month emergency fund.	
	Secure comprehensive health and life insurance coverage for the family.	
Duty and Responsibility	Develop a plan for debt repayment, focusing on loans like home loans or personal loans.	
	Set up dedicated funds for children's education through -	
Aspirations	Explore opportunities for real estate investment, considering homeownership aspirations.	
	Diversify investments through SIPs in mutual funds, PPF, direct stock portfolio or NPS for long-term growth.	
Contribution and Legacy	Obtain life insurance policies for financial protection and legacy planning.	
	Create a will and engage in estate planning to ensure a smooth transfer of assets.	
Tax Optimisation	Incorporate tax-efficient strategies into the financial plan, including deductions and exemptions.	
Retirement Planning	Contribute to retirement accounts, buy a pension plan, and use mutual fund SWP.	
Education and Skill Development	Invest in continuous education and skill development for professional growth.	
Philanthropy and Charitable Giving	Allocate a portion of the budget for charitable contributions.	

* * *

What have we learned so far from chapter 6:

16. _______________________________________

____

____

____

17. _______________________________________

____

____

____

18. _______________________________________

____

____

____

Note:

To deepen your understanding of the concepts covered in this chapter, please take the time to answer the following questions. Reflect on what you have learned and provide written responses to the open-ended questions. This exercise is designed to reinforce your knowledge and encourage you to apply the principles to your own financial planning.

What goal required the most money? Have you decided on your action plan for it?

____

____

Do I now have clarity on how to forecast my financial needs?

____

____

Do I now know where I should start my planning from?

____

____

Do I now have a plan of action?

____

____

Do I need to consult a financial planner or an adviser to start taking action?

____

____

phases of money

Chapter 7

3 Phases Of Money

Navigating personal finance can feel like a journey, and understanding the 3 main stages—Accumulation, Growth, and Preservation—can help you make smart decisions to secure your financial future.

In the vibrant city of Pune, there lived 3 friends: Rupiya, Rupee, and Sona. Each of them had their own perspective on the journey of money, reflecting the phases of accumulation, growth, and preservation with distribution, but in the context of the Indian culture and economy.

Let's begin with Rupiya. Rupiya was a diligent saver, much like his namesake, the Indian currency. Every day, he would carefully tuck away any spare change he had, no matter how small. Rupiya understood the value of accumulation in a country where every Rupee counts. He believed in the proverb "little drops make the mighty ocean" and diligently saved for his future, be it for his children's education or his retirement.

Next, there was Rupee. Rupee was an ambitious entrepreneur, always looking for opportunities to grow his wealth. He ventured into various business endeavours, from traditional trades to modern startups. The Rupee understood the importance of growth in a rapidly developing economy like India. He was not afraid to take risks, knowing that sometimes, fortune favours the bold. Through his hard work and determination, Rupee saw his wealth multiply, paving the way for a brighter future for himself and his family.

Lastly, there was Sona. Sona, which means gold in Hindi, was a symbol of wisdom and prosperity in Indian culture. Sona was a wise elder in the community, having lived through the ups and downs of the Indian economy. She believed in the principle of preservation with distribution, understanding that wealth must be carefully managed and shared for the greater good. Sona invested in gold, land, and other assets, ensuring financial security for herself and her loved ones. But she also had a generous heart, dedicating a portion of her wealth to charitable causes and believing in the importance of giving back to society.

As time passed, Rupiya, Rupee, and Sona continued their journey through the phases of money, each contributing in their own way to the economy of Pune.

Let's break down each stage in a way that's easy to follow.

7.1 Accumulation Phase

Think of the Accumulation Phase as the starting point of your financial journey. This is when you begin earning money, typically in the early stages of your career, and start building your financial foundation. Your main goal here is to save and invest consistently.

Key Objectives:

- **Building an Emergency Fund:** This is your financial safety net for unexpected expenses. Aim to save enough to cover 3 to 6 months' worth of living expenses in an easily accessible account.

- **Paying Off Debt:** Focus on eliminating high-interest debt, like credit card balances. Paying off debt frees up more money for savings and investments.

- **Starting Investments:** Begin investing in retirement accounts, such as a Annuities or pension plan. You might also consider stocks, bonds, or mutual funds. Starting early helps you benefit from compound interest.

- **Education and Skill Development:** Invest in your education and skills to boost your earning potential over time.

7.2 Growth Phase

Once you've got a solid financial base, you move into the Growth Phase. This is when you really start to maximise the returns on your accumulated assets, typically during your mid-career years.

Key Objectives:

- **Diversifying Investments:** Spread your investments across different asset classes (stocks, bonds, real estate) to manage risk and optimise returns.

- **Maximising Retirement Contributions:** Try to contribute the maximum allowed to retirement accounts to benefit from tax advantages and any employer matching contributions.

- **Long-Term Financial Planning:** Start planning for big future expenses, like your children's education, buying a home, or starting a business.

- **Risk Management:** Ensure you have adequate insurance coverage (health, life, disability) to protect your growing assets.

7.3 Preservation Phase

As you near retirement, your focus shifts to the Preservation Phase. Here, the goal is to protect your wealth and ensure your assets provide a stable income throughout your retirement years.

Key Objectives:

- **Creating a Retirement Plan:** Develop a detailed plan for withdrawing from your retirement accounts efficiently, considering things like required minimum distributions, like annuity or pension plans, SWP from mutual funds, post office schemes etc.

- **Adjusting Investment Strategy:** Shift to more conservative investments to protect your assets from market volatility. This might mean increasing your allocations to bonds or other fixed-income securities.

- **Estate Planning:** Update your will, set up trusts, and consider other estate planning tools to ensure your assets are distributed according to your wishes and to minimise estate taxes.

- **Health Care Planning:** Prepare for healthcare expenses by looking into long-term care insurance and understanding your Medicare benefits.

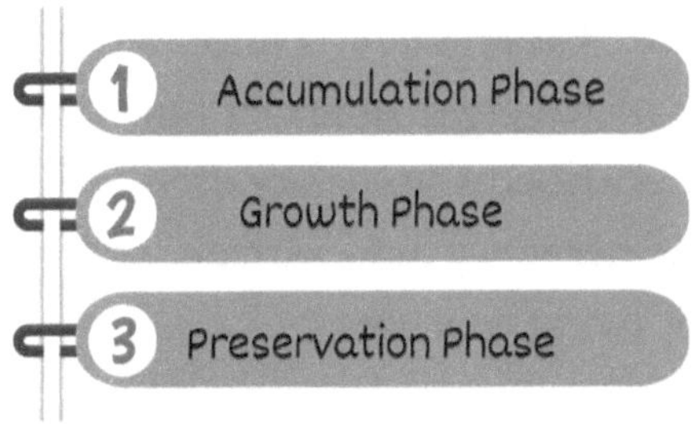

Understanding the Accumulation, Growth, and Preservation Phases of personal finance is key to achieving long-term financial stability. Each phase requires different strategies and focuses, but they're all connected on your journey to financial well-being. By recognising where you are and planning accordingly, you can make informed decisions to reach your financial goals and enjoy a secure and comfortable future.

Arjun, a young man from Mumbai, has a story that mirrors the financial journey many of us undertake. His path through the Accumulation Phase, Growth Phase, and Preservation Phase offers a practical example of how these stages unfold in real life.

7.4 Accumulation Phase: Building the Foundation

Arjun grew up in a modest household in Mumbai. After completing his engineering degree, he landed his first job at a local tech firm. Earning a steady income for the first time, Arjun embarked on the Accumulation Phase of his financial journey.

Key Activities:

- **Building an Emergency Fund**: Arjun knew the importance of having a financial safety net. He started by saving a portion of his salary each month, eventually building an emergency fund with enough money to cover 6 months of living expenses.

- **Paying Off Debt**: With student loans from his college days, Arjun made it a priority to pay down this debt quickly. He used a portion of his monthly earnings to make extra payments, reducing the interest over time.

- **Starting Investments**: Encouraged by his financially savvy colleague, Arjun opened a Public Provident Fund (PPF) account and started investing in a Systematic Investment Plan (SIP) in mutual funds. These early investments began to grow thanks to the power of compound interest.

- **Education and Skill Development**: Arjun didn't stop learning. He enrolled in online courses to enhance his technical skills, making him more valuable at work and opening doors for promotions and raises.

7.5 Growth Phase: Maximising Wealth

After several years, Arjun's career had progressed significantly. Now a senior engineer with a higher salary, he entered the Growth Phase, focusing on multiplying his wealth.

Key Activities:

- **Diversifying Investments**: With more disposable income, Arjun diversified his portfolio. He invested in stocks and real estate and even started a small business on the side with a friend.

- **Maximising Retirement Contributions**: Arjun made the maximum allowable contributions to his Employees' Provident Fund (EPF) and also invested in a National Pension System (NPS) account, taking full advantage of tax benefits. He even bought a pension plan for guaranteed returns.

- **Long-Term Financial Planning**: Arjun began planning for future milestones. He saved for a down payment on a flat in Mumbai, setting aside money each month. He also started an education fund for his younger sister, ensuring she wouldn't have to take on student loans.

- **Risk Management**: Understanding the importance of protecting his growing assets, Arjun purchased health insurance, life insurance, and disability insurance. This way, he safeguarded his financial future against unforeseen events.

7.6 Preservation Phase: Securing the Future

By the time Arjun reached his late 50s, he had amassed significant savings and investments. As he began contemplating retirement, he transitioned into the Preservation Phase, focusing on protecting and wisely using his wealth.

Key Activities:

- **Creating a Retirement Plan**: Arjun worked with a financial adviser to create a detailed retirement plan. They developed a strategy for withdrawing from his retirement accounts in the most tax-efficient manner, ensuring his savings would last throughout his retirement.

- **Adjusting Investment Strategy**: To reduce risk, Arjun shifted a portion of his investments into more stable, income-generating assets like government bonds and fixed deposits. This move protected his portfolio from market volatility.

- **Estate Planning**: Arjun updated his will and set up trusts to ensure his assets would be distributed according to his wishes. He wanted to provide for his family and support a few charities he cared about deeply.

- **Health Care Planning**: Preparing for potential healthcare costs, Arjun purchased long-term care insurance and reviewed his health insurance coverage to make sure it was adequate for his retirement years.

Arjun's journey from a young graduate in Mumbai to a financially secure retiree illustrates the importance of understanding and navigating the 3 phases of personal finance. His story shows that with discipline, planning, and continuous learning, anyone can achieve financial independence and security. Each phase required Arjun to adapt his strategies and focus on different financial goals, but the effort was well worth it, ensuring a comfortable and worry-free future.

Let's figure out where you are on your personal finance journey and what steps you should take next. There are 3 main phases: Accumulation, Growth, and Preservation. We'll identify which phase you're in and then look at some actions you can take to move forward.

Step 1: Identify Your Current Phase

Accumulation Phase

- Characteristics:
  - Just started earning an income
  - Building initial savings
  - Paying off debts (like student loans or credit cards)
  - Starting to invest

- Learning new skills for career growth. Questions to Ask Yourself:

  o Are you in the early stages of your career?

  o Do you have significant debt you're working to pay off?

  o Are you focused on building an emergency fund?

  o Are you just starting to invest or learning about investments?

Growth Phase

- Characteristics:

  o Steady and growing income

  o Established savings and investments

  o Diversifying your investment portfolio

  o Planning for long-term goals (like buying a house or saving for kids' education)

  o Making sure you have adequate insurance coverage

- Questions to Ask Yourself:

  o Have you been in your career for several years and seen salary increases?

  o Do you have a well-established emergency fund?

  o Are you investing regularly and diversifying your portfolio?

  o Are you planning for major future expenses?

Preservation Phase

- Characteristics:

    o Nearing retirement or already retired

    o Focused on preserving wealth rather than growing it

    o Adjusting investments to reduce risk

    o Planning for sustainable income during retirement

    o Estate and healthcare planning

- Questions to Ask Yourself:

    o Are you approaching or already in retirement?

    o Are you more concerned with preserving wealth than growing it?

    o Have you adjusted your investment strategy to be more conservative?

    o Are you planning how to withdraw from your retirement accounts efficiently?

Step 2: Take Action Based on Your Phase

Actions for the Accumulation Phase:

1. **Build an Emergency Fund**: Save enough to cover 3-6 months of living expenses.

2. **Pay Off High-Interest Debt**: Prioritise reducing debts like credit cards and personal loans.

3. **Start Investing**: Open retirement accounts (like PPF or EPF) and begin investing in mutual funds or SIPs.

4. **Enhance Skills**: Invest in education and skill development to increase your earning potential.

Actions for the Growth Phase:

1. **Diversify Investments**: Spread investments across different asset classes (stocks, bonds, real estate).

2. **Maximise Retirement Contributions**: Contribute the maximum to retirement accounts to benefit from tax advantages.

3. **Plan for Long-Term Goals**: Save for future milestones such as a home purchase, children's education, or starting a business.

4. **Ensure Adequate Insurance**: Review and update health, life, and disability insurance coverage.

Actions for the Preservation Phase:

1. **Create a Retirement Plan**: Develop a detailed plan for withdrawing from retirement accounts in a tax-efficient manner.

2. **Adjust Investment Strategy**: Shift towards more conservative investments to protect your wealth.

3. **Estate Planning**: Update your will, establish trusts, and make sure your estate planning documents are in order.

4. **Healthcare Planning**: Purchase long-term care insurance and ensure you have adequate health insurance coverage.

Take a moment to think about where you are right now. Are you just starting out and building your savings? Are you growing your wealth and planning for big future expenses? Or are you looking to preserve what you've built and ensure a comfortable retirement? Once you've identified your phase, use the action steps to guide your next moves. Keep revisiting and updating your plan as you move through different phases to stay on track towards your financial goals.

* * *

What have we learned so far from chapter 7?

19. _______________________________________

____

____

____

20. _______________________________________

____

____

____

21. _______________________________________

____

____

____

Note:

To deepen your understanding of the concepts covered in this chapter, please take the time to answer the following questions. Reflect on what you have learned and provide written responses to the open-ended questions. This exercise is designed to reinforce your knowledge and encourage you to apply the principles to your own financial planning.

Which phase do you believe you are currently in - Accumulation (Rupiya), Growth (Rupee), or Preservation (Sona?) And Why?

____

____

Do I now have clarity on how to find your money phase of life?

____

____

Do I now know what action steps different phases would require?

____

____

Do I now have a plan of action?

____

____

Do you need to get a review of your current phase and see if things are on track? Or talk to a financial expert?

____

____

Your Financial Journey Begins Now

As we conclude "Decoding Personal Finance," it's essential to reflect on the knowledge and tools you've gained throughout this book. You know what to do now, selecting the right plan, tool, investment basket, right adviser to help you through this is the next step. Remember that personal financial planning is not a one-time task, but a lifelong journey. By implementing the strategies and principles discussed in the previous chapters, you have taken a significant step towards financial empowerment and security.

Financial freedom is within your reach. With a solid understanding of the basics of personal finance, setting clear goals, creating a budget, managing debt, building an emergency fund, investing wisely, and protecting your assets, you are well-equipped to navigate the complexities of the Indian financial landscape.

However, always remember that each person's financial journey is unique. Your goals, circumstances, and risk tolerance may differ from others. Therefore, it's crucial to tailor the knowledge you've gained to fit your specific needs. Regularly reassess your financial situation, review your goals, and make adjustments, as necessary.

Beyond the pages of this playbook, seek additional resources and expand your financial knowledge. Stay informed about changes in tax laws, investment options, and financial regulations. Engage in discussions with professionals, attend seminars or workshops, and consider consulting a financial adviser when needed. Continuously learning and adapting will help you stay ahead in the ever-evolving world of personal finance.

Lastly, remember that financial well-being goes beyond mere numbers and accumulation of wealth. It's about aligning your financial decisions with your values, prioritising what truly matters to you, and finding the right balance between living for today and preparing for tomorrow. Use your financial freedom as a tool to create a meaningful and fulfilling life for yourself and your loved ones.

As you embark on your financial journey, remember that mistakes and setbacks are part of the process. Learn from them, remain persistent, and never lose sight of your goals. With determination, discipline, and the knowledge acquired from this playbook, you have the potential to achieve remarkable financial success and enjoy a life of abundance.

Congratulations on completing "Decoding Personal Finance." May this book serve as your guide and companion as you navigate the vast world of personal finance. Remember, your financial future is in your hands. Start taking action today and create a brighter tomorrow for yourself and your loved ones.

Wishing you all the best on your financial journey!

9 798889 446699